My Next Step
VISION BOARD
DREAM JOURNAL & PLANNER®
for Single Women
Desiring Marriage

A product of the
Coach in a Book Series™

*****

Creating answers and strategies
to help people get unstuck, succeed, and experience breakthrough.

Author: Tarsha L. Campbell
Certified Life & Empowerment Coach

www.TarshaCampbellEmpowers.com

ReadyForMyHusband.com

Copyright © 2022 Tarsha L. Campbell
ISBN 979-8-9865071-1-8

My Next Step Vision Board Dream Journal & Planner® and The Next Step Strategy®
are the registered trademarks of Tarsha Campbell Empowers, LLC

All Rights Reserved Worldwide

No part of this book may be reproduced or transmitted in any form or by any means, electronically or mechanically, including photocopying, recording, or by an information storage and retrieval system without permission in writing from the author and publisher of this book.

Unless otherwise indicated, all Scripture quotations are taken from the New King James Version®. Copyright © 1982 by Thomas Nelson. Used by permission. All rights reserved.

Scripture quotations marked (NLT) are taken from the Holy Bible, New Living Translation, Copyright © 1996, 2004, 2007 by Tyndale House Foundation. Used by permission of Tyndale House Publishers, Inc., Carol Stream, Illinois 60188.

Scripture quotations marked (CEV) are from the Contemporary English Version, Copyright © 1991, 1992, 1995 by American Bible Society. Used by permission.

Scripture quotations marked (BSB) are from The Holy Bible, Berean Study Bible, BSB, Copyright © 2016, 2020 by Bible Hub. Used by permission. All Rights Reserved Worldwide.

Noted definitions from *Dictionary*, Version 2.2.1 (194), Copyright © 2005–2016, Apple Inc., All rights reserved.

Book interior layout & cover design:
Tarsha L. Campbell

Published by:
DOMINIONHOUSE Publishing & Design, LLC
P.O. Box 681938 | Orlando, Florida 32868 | 407.703.4800
www.mydominionhouse.com

The Lord gave the Word: great was the company
of those who published it. (Psalm 68:11)

DEDICATION

This journal-planner is dedicated to every single woman who is ready to get ready to be found by her husband.

*"He who finds a wife finds
a treasure,
and he receives favor
from the Lord."*

- Proverbs 18:22 (NLT)

Table of Contents

Step 01
Introduction

Learn the purpose of this unique empowerment resource and the keys to a successful marriage.

Pg. 9

Step 02
Dear God

This is where your request for your husband should begin. Starting with a request to God ensures you will marry the man designed for you, and you designed for him.

Pg. 17

Step 03
My Vision Boards

Never underestimate the power of vision to make marital dreams come true. It's time to create vision boards to express your hopes and desires.

Pg. 23

Step 04
Clarifying your Core Values & Personal Creed

Clarifying your values and what you stand for will ensure you don't fall for anything or anyone.

Pg. 43

Step 05
Identifying Your Strengths & Barriers

Let's spend time identifying your strengths, weaknesses, opportunities, and threats (SWOT), as well as the barriers you are facing when it comes to being found by your future husband.

Pg. 55

Step 06
Steps to Get Ready for Marriage

It's time to take the necessary steps and pinpoint items you must work on to spiritually, psychologically, emotionally, relationally, and financially prepare for marriage.

Pg. 65

Step 07
The Attraction Factor

Where do you stand when it comes to outer & inner beauty? Are you on point, do you need some tweaks, or do you need a complete makeover?

Pg. 73

Step 08
Husband Magnet

Are you a husband magnet? Have you identified the positive & negative qualities you possess that would attract or repel your future husband?

Pg. 85

Table of Contents

Step 09
Financially Fit & Fine

A financially prepared woman is an attractive wife-to-be to a wise man searching for his wife. Are you financially fit & fine?

Pg. 89

Step 10
Dear Future Husband Letters

Keep your dreams alive, and by faith, write letters to your future husband to express your heart to him.

Pg. 99

Step 11
My Bucket Lists

My Engagement Bucket List
My Wedding Bucket List
My Honeymoon Bucket List
My Marriage Bucket List

Pg. 109

Step 12
My Hope Chest

Preparation is key. Write down things you'll need at the start of your marriage.

Pg. 117

Step 13
My Vow to Purity

Purity matters. Write your promise to God, yourself, and your future husband.

Pg. 123

Step 14
31 Days of Affirmations

It's time to align your thoughts and words with what you envision by writing affirmations about your future as a married woman.

Pg. 129

Step 15
Scripture Meditation for Preparation

Let's meditate upon Scriptures to help you prepare for and approach marriage by studying how God views and designed it.

Pg. 141

Step 16
Dreaming Ahead:
Planning for Your Wedding Day

You've got yourself all ready for your future husband to find you. Don't stop dreaming and envisioning. Now plan what you will need for your wedding day.

Pg. 159

Table of Contents

Step 17

Advice for a Happy Married Life

Go to those who know. Get advice from high-quality and high-standard wives and men who can help you prepare for a successful marriage.

Pg. 205

Step 18

I'm Glad You Found Me

By faith, compose a prayer of thanksgiving and a declaration of gratitude because you have been found by your beloved husband.

Pg. 213

Meet the Author

Pg. 216

"God will bless you to the degree you are prepared."

— Pastor John Jenkins

"You can want a husband and still not be desperate. Making peace with the process is contentment."

- Bishop T.D. Jakes

CHAPTER
01

Introduction

"...I have deduced that there are certain things that must be in order in your life to make way for you to attract, meet, and marry the man whom God has prepared for you."

— Coach Tarsha Campbell

INTRODUCTION

Dear Single Sister,

Do you desire to be married? Do you dream about spending the rest of your life with the one you love?

Proverbs 18:22 (NKJV) says, "He who finds a wife finds a good thing, and obtains favor from the Lord." I love how the New Living Translation (NTL) translates this verse: "The man who finds a wife finds a treasure, and he receives favor from the LORD." From both of these translations, we can clearly see that marriage is a good thing and a God thing.

Marriage can be a wonderful part of one's life, and it is my wish that every woman who desires to be married can experience the beauty of this special covenant, established by God, between husband and wife. I have often wondered, though: are there any prerequisites required that lead to the exclusive convergence of two lives and hearts—in Holy Matrimony and sweet union—based on God's grand design for marriage?

What most stands out to me in Proverbs 18:22 is the first part of that Scripture, which states, "He who finds a wife…" I don't know about you, but the two key words, "find" and "wife," seem to scream for my attention. Are you ready for your future husband to find his wife? I strongly believe that, in order to attract and be found by the man who is to be your husband, you must

Introduction

already be a "wife." *In my opinion, this is a "key" prerequisite to marriage that every single woman desiring to be married should zero in on.*

Having seen it play out in my own life, as well as in the lives of former single women who are now happily married, I have deduced that there are certain things that must be in order in your life to make way for you to attract, meet, and marry the man whom God has prepared for you. Are you ready? In your present state, can you be recognized and identified as a wife? I've concluded that, while there may be tons of single women out there, a wise and suitable man (and I stress *"wise and suitable man"*) searching for the person with whom to spend the rest of his life in Holy Matrimony is searching for not just a woman but a "wife."

With that point established, as a single woman desiring marriage—and as a single woman living with a biblical worldview—it's important that you prepare for marriage. I feel it's necessary that you develop the mindset of a wife long before you actually walk down the aisle to become a wife. Preparation is key. It puts you on the path to being "found" by your future husband, who is searching for "his wife," with the ultimate goal of having a successful marriage.

Keys to a Successful Marriage

A successful marriage is a two-way street. It's not about taking and receiving all the time. Rather, it involves two lives merging and the willingness to give unselfishly to one's spouse.

A successful marriage that presents an opportunity for both parties to be satisfied requires a conscious effort on the part of both individuals. Marriage is a life of personal sacrifice built upon a solid foundation of love. This type of love transcends blazing physical attraction, sweet romantic interludes, and passionate sexual escapades. It also includes being willing to give of yourself spiritually and emotionally, as well as bringing your life resources together to enable you to prosper as a married couple.

Introduction

I feel that a successful marriage eludes many because one or both parties are ill-prepared for a life joined in matrimony. Inadequate preparation, or a complete lack thereof, may leave you open to unnecessary heartache and pain, or even the possibility of a failed marriage.

To help you avoid all the negative aspects of connecting with the wrong person, or even missing the opportunity to be found by the man destined to be your future husband, I have created this unique vision board dream journal and planner for single women desiring to be married.

As a successfully married woman and empowerment coach, I've designed coaching and personal development worksheets to help you work through getting spiritually, psychologically, emotionally, relationally, physically, and financially prepared for marriage and the role of a wife. The goal of this empowerment resource is to set you on a path for entry into a beautiful life of Holy Matrimony and marital bliss. After 34 years of being happily married, I can honestly say that this is possible.

Can I honestly say that every day of my marriage has been rosy? No, but I can say that it was the personal evaluation, inventory, and work I did to prepare myself for marriage that helped me maturely handle the rough patches. As a result of this preparation, the way was opened for my spouse and I to emerge successfully on the other side of the rough times with our love, commitment, and mutual respect intact. The bonus is that we have grown even more intimately connected on all levels and more deeply in love with each other. I can honestly say that it's been a life of sweet love and divine fulfillment for both of us… And I am anticipating many more years of happiness with my beloved.

Do you want to create an opportunity to experience similar marital happiness? I believe it's possible, but I feel that it all starts with personally preparing your heart, mind, and life for your future spouse and marriage.

It starts with having a realistic vision of yourself as a wife. I strongly believe that you have to start envisioning yourself as a wife, thinking like a wife,

Introduction

planning like a wife, and preparing yourself to be a wife before you actually become a wife to the husband God has prepared and predestined for you.

Key components of your preparation should include living your life based on an honorable life creed and respectable core values that will make you irresistible to your Mr. Right. Have you clarified these items? Have you established the non-negotiables in your life to ensure you will not lower your standards and settle for just any man who shows you attention?

Receiving attention isn't a bad thing, but how it's garnered and who it's coming from can initiate and set the tone for two outcomes. One outcome involves productive interactions and a meaningful relationship, while the second outcome involves the type of attention that can lead to nonproductive interactions and an unfulfilling relationship with the wrong guy (or guys, if you think back over the course of your life). The second outcome can potentially leave a bad taste in your mouth and negatively reverberate throughout your entire life. I want you to avoid this scenario and to prepare for productive outcomes, ultimately including a successful marriage.

This unique empowerment resource is all about helping you get grounded and establishing a strong foundation for your life as a wife. It showcases The Next Step Strategy®, a step-by-step strategy designed to help you prepare to be a wife. Each component of this journal-planner is specifically and specially designed to help you set yourself up to attract the husband perfectly designed for you, and you for him. I strongly believe that God will bless you to the degree that you are prepared.

You might say, "What and who are going to help my future husband be prepared for me?" My answer is to leave that to God. Allow Him to use you and the engaging components of this unique resource to set in motion, as engineered by the Holy Spirit in the spirit, the heart preparation of the right man destined to find you to be his wife. This is what you want, right? The Holy Spirit to be at the forefront, leading, guiding, and preparing you and your future husband for each other? If this is what you desire, let's get started on the exciting journey of preparing you to envision yourself as a wife, as well as the journey of aligning things in your life so you will be more attractive and undeniably irresistible to your future husband. He's coming to find you, and if you put in the work, this empowerment resource will help you get ready for him and position you to be found. Let's go!

— Coach Tarsha

"...God is the one who has your future in His hands. It's by His divine power, intentions, and intervention that He can make your desire and dream to marry your reality."

- Coach Tarsha Campbell

CHAPTER
02

Dear God...

"God cares about what you care about, including your desire to marry and being found by your future husband."

- Coach Tarsha Campbell

Dear God...

More than anyone besides you, God is the one who has your future in His hands. It's by His divine power, intentions, and intervention that He can make your desire and dream to marry your reality.

Knowing this is the case, don't you think it would be a wise decision to start preparing to become the wife your future husband is looking for? The first step of this process is to express to God your heart's desires concerning marriage and being found by the right person.

Psalm 37:4-5 (NKJV) states:

> 4 Delight yourself also in the LORD, And He shall give you the desires of your heart. 5 Commit your way to the LORD, Trust also in Him, And He shall bring it to pass.

Based on the principles espoused by this Scripture passage, I believe that when you as a single woman take delight in pleasing God (which means seeking your happiness and fulfillment in Him), He will move on your behalf and be the prime catalyst in fulfilling the desires you seek. This definitely sounds like a win-win situation to me.

Dear God...

With that being expressed, use the space provided below to write God a letter, believing and knowing that He cares about what you care about, including your desire to marry and be found by your future husband.

You are also encouraged to write the letter from the perspective that God knows what's best for you. This means truly taking delight in the Lord and committing your ways to Him. Wanting what He wants always yields superlative results.

Dear God,

_____

_____

_____

_____

_____

_____

_____

_____

_____

_____

Dear God...

"Expectation is the breeding ground for dreams and visions to come true!"

- Coach Tarsha Campbell

CHAPTER
03

My Vision Boards

*"When you can see what
God sees for your life,
it makes a world of difference
and gives you hope."*

- Coach Tarsha Campbell

The Power of Vision & Vision Boards

Vision is a powerful thing! Vision gives you the power to look beyond your current situation and see into the future. Everything you see around you started with a vision. The houses we live in, the cars we drive, the technology we use—the list goes on and on. Vision is the undeniable force that allows you to step out of today, venture into tomorrow to view future possibilities, and then step back into the present to recreate what you have seen. Isn't that fascinating?

In Genesis 1:26-27, God speaks of making man (and woman) in His image and likeness. Without a doubt, the ability to envision what could be is one of the characteristics that make us like Him. As descendants of the Divine Creator, we all have the power to envision what could be and then take the necessary actions to make that a reality.

From the positive relationships we long for, the material things we need, and the lifestyles we want and dream about to the finances that fund the currents of our lives, including the health and well-being we desire, all the critical elements of life can be realized first through the power of vision.

This book was designed to help you harness this power by encouraging you to write and display your visions, continually keep them at the forefront of your mind, and intentionally take steps every day to work in cooperation with

God's plan and purpose for your life so you can bring your God-given visions to fruition. Use this book to dream and envision BIG things. Make BOLD and CALCULATED moves as you plan your future as a married woman. Finally, have UNWAVERING faith that your hopes, dreams, and God-ordained visions will become your reality. It's absolutely possible. By God's grace, you can realize and see the manifestation of what you envision!

THE PURPOSE OF THIS JOURNAL-PLANNER
•••
WHAT YOU SHOULD KNOW ABOUT THIS RESOURCE

When you know why something was created, that something can better serve you. This book is all about helping you stay focused on your God-given visions so that you don't lose sight of them. This book isn't meant to make your visions, dreams, and desires into idols in your life. Rather, it is meant to encourage you not to neglect God's overall vision and dream for you, which is summed up in Jeremiah 29:11 (KJV):

> For I know the thoughts that I think toward you,
> saith the Lord, thoughts of peace, and not of evil,
> to give you an expected end.

It is God's desire to give you a beautiful, fulfilling life full of peace, love, and prosperity. Will you dare to envision what He sees for you?

Here is something to think about when it comes to executing your vision.
•••
The word execute has two meanings.
That being the case, there are two ways to <u>execute</u> a vision.

to kill by putting something to death
--or--
to carry something out to completion

How will you choose to execute your God-given visions and prepare yourself to be found by your future husband? The choice is yours.

MY VISION BOARD #1 – MY LIFE AS A SINGLE WOMAN

Use a glue stick or tape and place images that represent what you envision for this part of your life.

MY VISION BOARD #1 – MY LIFE AS A SINGLE WOMAN

My Vision Board #2 – My Future as a Married Woman

Use a glue stick or tape and place images that represent what you envision for this part of your life.

MY VISION BOARD #2 - MY FUTURE AS A MARRIED WOMAN

I'm Ready

MY VISION BOARD #3 – MY IDEAL MATE/FUTURE HUSBAND

Use a glue stick or tape and place images that represent what you envision for this part of your life.

MY VISION BOARD #3 – MY IDEAL MATE/FUTURE HUSBAND

I'm Ready

MY VISION BOARD #4 – OUR IDEAL LIFE TOGETHER

Use a glue stick or tape and place images that represent what you envision for this part of your life.

I'm Ready

MY VISION BOARD #4 – OUR IDEAL LIFE TOGETHER

My Vision Board #5 – Our Future Financial Life

Use a glue stick or tape and place images that represent what you envision for this part of your life.

I'm Ready

MY VISION BOARD #5 – OUR FUTURE FINANCIAL LIFE

Use a glue stick or tape and place images that represent what you envision for this part of your life.

My Vision Board #6 – Our Ideal Wedding

I'm Ready

MY VISION BOARD #6 – OUR IDEAL WEDDING

MY VISION BOARD #7 – OUR IDEAL FAMILY LIFE

Use a glue stick or tape and place images that represent what you envision for this part of your life.

I'm Ready

MY VISION BOARD #7 – OUR IDEAL FAMILY LIFE

"If you don't identify what you
believe and stand for, you are subject
to lower your standards
while waiting to marry."

- Coach Tarsha Campbell

CHAPTER
04

Clarifying Your Core Values & Personal Creed

"Your core values help bring balance into your life. They empower you to build a strong and sustaining foundation for a successful life that may include marriage."

- Coach Tarsha Campbell

Clarifying Your Core Values

When preparing yourself for marriage, you should not overlook the step of identifying your core values, which consist of the anchoring beliefs that establish the foundation for your life and experiences.

Your core values help bring balance into your life. They empower you to build a strong and sustaining foundation for a successful life that may include marriage.

Your identified core values serve as a gauge in all aspects of your personal life and will be vitally useful when you move into a relationship that could lead to marriage. They are the non-negotiable characteristics and attributes that help you make critical life decisions and are particularly important during the dating and premarital phases. Your core values will also impact your future marriage and establish a solid foundation upon which you and your future husband can build your lives.

Clarifying Your Core Values & Personal Creed

Read over the following list. Check the core values which you possess and which best describe you. Use the extra lines at the end of the list to add core values not listed. To avoid becoming overwhelmed, limit your list to 10 to 15 words.

MY NOTES

- ☐ Acceptance
- ☐ Ambition
- ☐ Authenticity
- ☐ Beauty (attractiveness)
- ☐ Compassion
- ☐ Competency
- ☐ Competitiveness
- ☐ Consistency
- ☐ Dedication
- ☐ Determination
- ☐ Diligence
- ☐ Elegance
- ☐ Empathy
- ☐ Encouragement
- ☐ Excellence
- ☐ Family
- ☐ Fidelity
- ☐ Forgiveness
- ☐ Freedom
- ☐ Fulfillment
- ☐ Fun
- ☐ Honesty
- ☐ Honor
- ☐ Humility
- ☐ Improvement
- ☐ Independence
- ☐ Influence
- ☐ Ingenuity
- ☐ Inspiration

Clarifying Your Core Values & Personal Creed

- ☐ Integrity
- ☐ Intelligence
- ☐ Joy
- ☐ Kindness
- ☐ Love
- ☐ Legacy
- ☐ Marriage
- ☐ Mastery
- ☐ Mentoring
- ☐ Money
- ☐ Orderliness
- ☐ Organization
- ☐ Partnership
- ☐ Peace
- ☐ Persistence
- ☐ Power
- ☐ Presentation
- ☐ Productivity
- ☐ Progress
- ☐ Purity
- ☐ Quietness
- ☐ Relationship
- ☐ Respect
- ☐ Rest
- ☐ Risk taking
- ☐ Safety
- ☐ Self-esteem
- ☐ Self-control

- ☐ Self-development
- ☐ Serenity
- ☐ Service
- ☐ Sexual intimacy
- ☐ Sexual fulfillment
- ☐ Significance
- ☐ Spiritual growth
- ☐ Steadfastness
- ☐ Success
- ☐ Submission
- ☐ Tact
- ☐ Tolerance
- ☐ Tranquility
- ☐ Trust
- ☐ Truth
- ☐ Understanding
- ☐ Validation
- ☐ Vigilance
- ☐ Vitality
- ☐ Winning/conquering
- ☐ Worship/reverence
- ☐ Work

_____

_____

_____

_____

"Your creed helps you govern your conduct and behavior. It conveys the standard by which you will consciously choose to live your life."

- Coach Tarsha Campbell

Composing Your Personal Creed

Now that you have pinpointed your dominant core values, let's take it a step further and compose your life creed. A creed is a clear and concise articulation of the established beliefs that serve to guide and gauge your actions. Your creed helps you govern your conduct and behavior. It conveys the standard by which you will consciously choose to live your life. To help you see what I mean, check out my personal creed based on my identified core values.

Quick Note: I live my life from a Biblical and Christian worldview, and this is reflected in the language used in my creed. Each person's creed will reflect their own worldview.

In living my life and working to accomplish my divine life purpose, I will—with the strength and guidance of the Holy Spirit and with ongoing consultation from those whose feedback I value—commit myself to consistently:

a. Honor God with my life
b. Live according to His word
c. Love others as I love myself
d. Abide in faith and purity
e. Be a living witness in all I do and say
f. Walk in peace with all men

Clarifying Your Core Values & Personal Creed

g. Put God first spiritually, physically, and financially
h. Strive for excellence in all I do
i Walk authentically before God and man
j. Live my life to the fullest in alignment with God's purpose for me
k. Value my marriage vows and always love, honor, and respect my husband
l. Honor and respect my fellow human beings
m. Allow self-control to guide my actions and attitude
n. Seek to grow spiritually, emotionally, and intellectually
o. Commit myself to helping others grow, advance, and prosper
p. Leave a positive legacy for the benefit of my children and the world

---

Compose Your Life Creed

Now it's your turn. Compose your life creed using the following space. Once your life creed is written, make it a practice to read it frequently and live by it consistently.

Clarifying Your Core Values & Personal Creed

MY LIFE CREED

My Standard

Clarifying Your Core Values & Personal Creed

My Life Creed

My Standard

Clarifying Your Core Values & Personal Creed

MY LIFE CREED

My Standard

"Your strengths and barriers can either make you or break you."

- Coach Tarsha Campbell

CHAPTER 05

Identifying Your Strengths & Barriers

> *"When you don't know what's working for or against you, it's hard to gauge where you stand in reaching your goals and realizing what you envision."*
>
> - Coach Tarsha Campbell

Identifying Your Strengths & Barriers

As a single woman desiring marriage, it's important to identify the personal strengths that could be an asset to you when preparing to be a wife to your future spouse. Also, it's crucial to identify the barriers that could hinder you from being an excellent wife. So, let's conduct a SWOT analysis to help you identify the internal and external factors that serve as pros and cons working for or against you. Doing so will allow you to make the appropriate changes, adjustments, and re-tooling deemed necessary for you to see the manifestation of your desires, visions, dreams, and goals.

Strengths: The positive assets, capabilities, knowledge, and attributes you possess that help you excel as a person and could be advantageous to you as a wife.

Weaknesses: The negative tendencies, assets, and attributes you possess that could be problematic to you as a wife.

Opportunities: The favorable factors, circumstances, and elements you have access to that will help you prepare to be a great wife to your future husband.

Threats: The situations, factors, and circumstances that could cause potential damage, harm, misalignment, and misfortune to you as you prepare to be a wife.

Identifying Your Strengths & Barriers

STRENGTHS

Use the following prompts to identify your SWOT: **S**trengths, **W**eaknesses, **O**pportunities, and **T**hreats.

List 5–10 things that would be your strengths as a wife.

☐ Example: I'm a great cook and enjoy cooking for others.

☐ _____

☐ _____

☐ _____

☐ _____

☐ _____

☐ _____

☐ _____

☐ _____

☐ _____

WEAKNESSES

List 5–10 things that would be your weaknesses as a wife.

- ☐ Example: I like living alone. I don't like sharing my space with others.
- ☐
- ☐
- ☐
- ☐
- ☐
- ☐
- ☐
- ☐
- ☐

OPPORTUNITIES

List 5–10 things that could be opportunities to prepare you to be an excellent wife to your future husband.

☐ Example: I'm being mentored by awesome married women.

☐ _____

☐ _____

☐ _____

☐ _____

☐ _____

☐ _____

☐ _____

☐ _____

☐ _____

THREATS

List 5–10 things that could threaten (hinder) you from becoming an excellent wife to your future husband.

☐ Example: I think all men are dogs and can't be trusted.

☐ _____

☐ _____

☐ _____

☐ _____

☐ _____

☐ _____

☐ _____

☐ _____

☐ _____

Identifying Your Strengths & Barriers

LIMITING BELIEFS

List 1–2 limiting beliefs that could hold you back from becoming an excellent wife to your future husband.

☐ _____

☐ _____

Where did these beliefs come from?

How can you overcome them?

CULTURAL BARRIERS

What are some cultural barriers you may have to deal with when embarking upon marriage if you marry outside your current culture?

"Each intentional step you make puts you closer to where you want to be."

- Coach Tarsha Campbell

CHAPTER
06

STEPS TO GET READY FOR MARRIAGE

Steps to Get Ready for Marriage

STEP 1

What do I need to work on spiritually?
- What do I know about myself?

Reflections:

How do my trusted family members or friends see me in this area?

Steps to Get Ready for Marriage

STEP 2

What do I need to work on psychologically (i.e., regarding my mental state and mindset)?

- What do I know about myself?

Reflections:

How do my trusted family members or friends see me in this area?

Steps to Get Ready for Marriage

STEP 3

What do I need to work on emotionally?
- What do I know about myself?

Reflections:

How do my trusted family members or friends see me in this area?

Steps to Get Ready for Marriage

STEP 4

What do I need to work on relationally (i.e., in my relationships)?
- What do I know about myself?

Reflections:

How do my trusted family members or friends see me in this area?

Steps to Get Ready for Marriage

STEP 5

What do I need to work on financially?
- What do I know about myself?

Reflections:

How do my trusted family members or friends see me in this area?

Quotes & Notes:

"When I take the steps to get myself in order, I open the door to come in alignment with God's will and all He has for me."

"Regardless of the importance that some may attach to it, being attractive is a key factor in gaining the attention of your future husband."

- Coach Tarsha Campbell

CHAPTER
07

THE ATTRACTION FACTOR

"Some women feel that 'fixing up' is not important...However, this doesn't negate the fact that men are drawn to and seek out attractive women."

- Coach Tarsha Campbell

THE ATTRACTION FACTOR

Regardless of the importance that some may attach to it, being attractive is a key factor in gaining the attention of your future husband. This fact is significant and holds true. It's widely known, and should not be dismissed, that men respond and are drawn to attractive women. Whether a woman's attractiveness is related to her outer beauty, inner beauty, undeniable confidence, or a combination of all three, men respond to, desire, and seek an attractive woman when companionship, a romantic relationship, or marriage is their goal.

Some women feel that "fixing up" is not important, while others may not find the "Attraction Factor" important, conveying their scorn verbally and/or through their attitude: "Well, they (men) are just going to have to accept me as I am."

If you, a single woman, hold either or both of the two attitudes just mentioned, you are certainly entitled to your opinion. However, this doesn't negate the fact that men are drawn to and seek out attractive women. That being said, it will be key to focus on and shore up your Attraction Factor so that you attract the future husband who is searching for you. Use the following Attraction Factor worksheet to pinpoint areas where you are doing fine or where you think you can improve.

OUTER BEAUTY

•••

How am I doing in these areas?

MY HAIRSTYLE

Note: If necessary, you can also ask a trusted family member or friend to help you identify what you need to work on in the following areas. Preferably, find some someone who is knowledgeable and serves as a great example.

☐ Excellent
☐ Needs to improve some
☐ Needs a complete makeover

Add personal notes, an action plan, and sample photos of the looks you like or desire to have.

MY SKIN/MAKE-UP

☐ Excellent
☐ Needs to improve some
☐ Needs a complete makeover

Add personal notes, an action plan, and sample photos of the looks you like or desire to have.

My Wardrobe

☐ Excellent
☐ Needs to improve some
☐ Needs a complete makeover

Add personal notes, an action plan, and sample photos of the looks you like or desire to have.

MY WEIGHT

☐ I'm at my ideal weight
☐ I'm below my ideal weight
☐ I'm overweight & want to change

Add personal notes, an action plan, and sample photos of the looks you like or desire to have.

DO I NEED A COMPLETE MAKEOVER?

☐ Yes
☐ A few tweaks won't hurt
☐ I'm ready for something new

Add personal notes, an action plan, and sample photos of the looks you like or desire to have.

People who can help me with this:

HAIR:

MAKE-UP:

WARDROBE:

WEIGHT:

INNER BEAUTY

•••

Where do you stand when it comes to inner beauty?

This is equally important, if not more important, than outer beauty and definitely should not be overlooked when preparing to be found by your future husband.

Check the positive qualities you possess:

- ☐ Adaptable
- ☐ Authentic
- ☐ Bold
- ☐ Captivating
- ☐ Cheery
- ☐ Compassionate
- ☐ Confident
- ☐ Courageous
- ☐ Creative
- ☐ Disciplined
- ☐ Dynamic
- ☐ Faithful
- ☐ Grateful
- ☐ Happy
- ☐ Helpful
- ☐ Honorable
- ☐ Humble
- ☐ Intelligent
- ☐ Joyful
- ☐ Kind
- ☐ Lovely
- ☐ Loving
- ☐ Meek
- ☐ Motivated
- ☐ Optimistic
- ☐ Resilient
- ☐ Resourceful
- ☐ Responsible
- ☐ Righteous
- ☐ Sane
- ☐ Self-assured
- ☐ Stable
- ☐ Supportive
- ☐ Sweet
- ☐ Teachable
- ☐ Tenacious
- ☐ Trustworthy
- ☐ Truthful
- ☐ Wise

INNER BEAUTY

• • •

This next part may be hard to face, but it's necessary to address it. Check those negative qualities you possess that could be complete turn-offs and might repel your future husband, deterring him from finding you or getting to know you. Include all the qualities you need to work on and then work on improving in these areas.

Check the negative qualities you possess:

- ☐ Aggravating
- ☐ Angry
- ☐ Bitter
- ☐ Bossy
- ☐ Cheater
- ☐ Compassionless
- ☐ Contentious
- ☐ Controlling
- ☐ Crazy
- ☐ Critical
- ☐ Crude
- ☐ Fearful
- ☐ Foolish
- ☐ Gloomy
- ☐ Hurtful
- ☐ Inconsistent
- ☐ Know-it-all
- ☐ Liar
- ☐ Manipulative
- ☐ Moody/temperamental
- ☐ Negative disposition
- ☐ Pessimistic
- ☐ Prideful
- ☐ Rude
- ☐ Sad
- ☐ Selfish
- ☐ Timid
- ☐ Unforgiving
- ☐ Unmotivated
- ☐ Unteachable
- ☐ Whiny

GET HELP

Find a trusted family member or friend and ask them to help you identify the positive and negative qualities you possess when it comes to inner beauty.

"The qualities, disposition, and habits you possess can either attract your future husband like a magnet or repel him. What he encounters is strictly up to you."

- Coach Tarsha Campbell

CHAPTER
08

HUSBAND MAGNET

HUSBAND MAGNET - ATTRACT

•••

Use the information you found out about yourself in the previous exercises and write down the qualities, disposition, and habits you possess that will attract your future husband.

HUSBAND MAGNET - REPEL
•••
Use the information you found out about yourself in the previous exercises and write down the qualities, disposition, and habits you possess that will repel your future husband.

"A financially prepared woman is an attractive wife-to-be to a wise man searching for his wife."

- Coach Tarsha Campbell

CHAPTER
09

FINANCIALLY FIT & FINE

"A wise and suitable mate will look at your financial stewardship records to gauge where you two may be in the future financially. Will he like what he sees?"

- Coach Tarsha Campbell

FINANCIALLY FIT & FINE

A big part of preparing to marry that is commonly overlooked by the dreamy-eyed single woman desiring to marry is asking the question, "Am I financially fit & fine?" Will your future husband-to-be find you in a suitable financial position, in the sense of having a good handle on your money and financial destiny?

Too often, I've seen and heard single women desiring marriage imagine being swept off their feet by a financial knight in shining armor. Blinded by their lofty expectations and raging desires, these women fail to see that their expected knight is looking for a future wife who isn't mismanaging her money, drowning in debt, or in a financial situation that looks like it's about to self-destruct any minute, taking down anyone in close proximity.

I believe and know for a fact that being financially fit & fine can be an attractive feature to a wise man looking for his future wife. You do want a wise man, right? Not a man only attracted to your outer appearance but a wise man who has a good handle on his money and financial destiny and is on the lookout for a financially savvy, Proverbs 31 kind of wife (I encourage you to study that Scripture passage). This type of wife is the type a wise man can partner with and build financial wealth with for a lifetime. Are you that kind of woman? Are you ready to be that type of wife? Will your future husband find you financially fit and fine? Or will your financial situation send him running the other way?

My Financial Goals & Monthly Budget

Let's work on being financially fit & fine by getting into the practice of establishing financial goals and having a monthly vision for your money, which is called a budget.

What I want to achieve Financially:

In 1 year:

In 2-4 years:

What I Want to Achieve Financially:

In 5-7 Years:

In 8-10 Years:

NOTES:

Financially Fit & Fine

EXPENSES: BILLS/PAYMENTS	JAN	FEB	MAR	APR
TOTAL				
MONTHLY INCOME				
MONTHLY SAVINGS				
MONTHLY EXPENSES				
MONEY LEFT				

Financially Fit & Fine

EXPENSES: BILLS/PAYMENTS	MAY	JUN	JUL	AUG
TOTAL				
MONTHLY INCOME				
MONTHLY SAVINGS				
MONTHLY EXPENSES				
MONEY LEFT				

Financially Fit & Fine

EXPENSES: BILLS/PAYMENTS	SEPT	OCT	NOV	DEC
TOTAL				
MONTHLY INCOME				
MONTHLY SAVINGS				
MONTHLY EXPENSES				
MONEY LEFT				

Quotes & Notes:

"Empowered women master their money, instead of their money mastering them."

"Expressing the desires of your heart is one of the first steps to realizing your dreams and seeing your visions manifest. Believe and dream out loud."

- Coach Tarsha Campbell

CHAPTER 10

Dear Future Husband Letters

Dear Future Husband Letters

•••
Let's dream out loud; by faith, write a letter to your future husband on the following subject:
I'm glad you found me.

Dear Future Husband,

Let's dream out loud; by faith, write a letter to your future husband on the following subject:
My promise while dating.

Dear Future Husband,

•••
Let's dream out loud; by faith, write a letter to your future husband on the following subject:
What our first year will be like.

Dear Future Husband,

•••
Let's dream out loud; by faith, write a letter to your future husband on the following subject: **Our future life together.**

Dear Future Husband,

•••
Let's dream out loud; by faith, write a letter to your future husband on the following subject: **Our financial destiny.**

Dear Future Husband,

•••
Let's dream out loud; by faith, write a letter to your future husband on the following subject:
Our home life together.

Dear Future Husband,

•••
Let's dream out loud; by faith, write a letter to your future husband on the following subject: **Our kids and family.**

Dear Future Husband,

Dear Future Husband Letters

•••
Let's dream out loud; by faith, write a letter to your future husband on the following subject:
What you mean to me.

Dear Future Husband,

*"If you can dream it, plan it,
and take proper actions,
it can become your reality.
Tomorrow belongs to you."*

- Coach Tarsha Campbell

CHAPTER
11

MY BUCKET LISTS

My Bucket Lists

Use the space below to list what you would like to do with your future husband during your engagement.

To Try

_____
_____
_____
_____
_____

To See

_____
_____
_____
_____
_____

To Visit

_____
_____
_____
_____
_____

To Learn

_____
_____
_____
_____
_____

My Bucket Lists

•••
Use the space below to list what you would like to do with your future husband for or during your wedding.

TO TRY

_____
_____
_____
_____
_____

TO SEE

_____
_____
_____
_____
_____

TO VISIT

_____
_____
_____
_____
_____

TO LEARN

_____
_____
_____
_____
_____

My Bucket Lists

To Try	To See

To Visit	To Learn

My Bucket Lists

•••
Use the space below to list what you would like to do with your future husband during the first 6 months you're married.

To Try

To See

To Visit

To Learn

My Bucket Lists

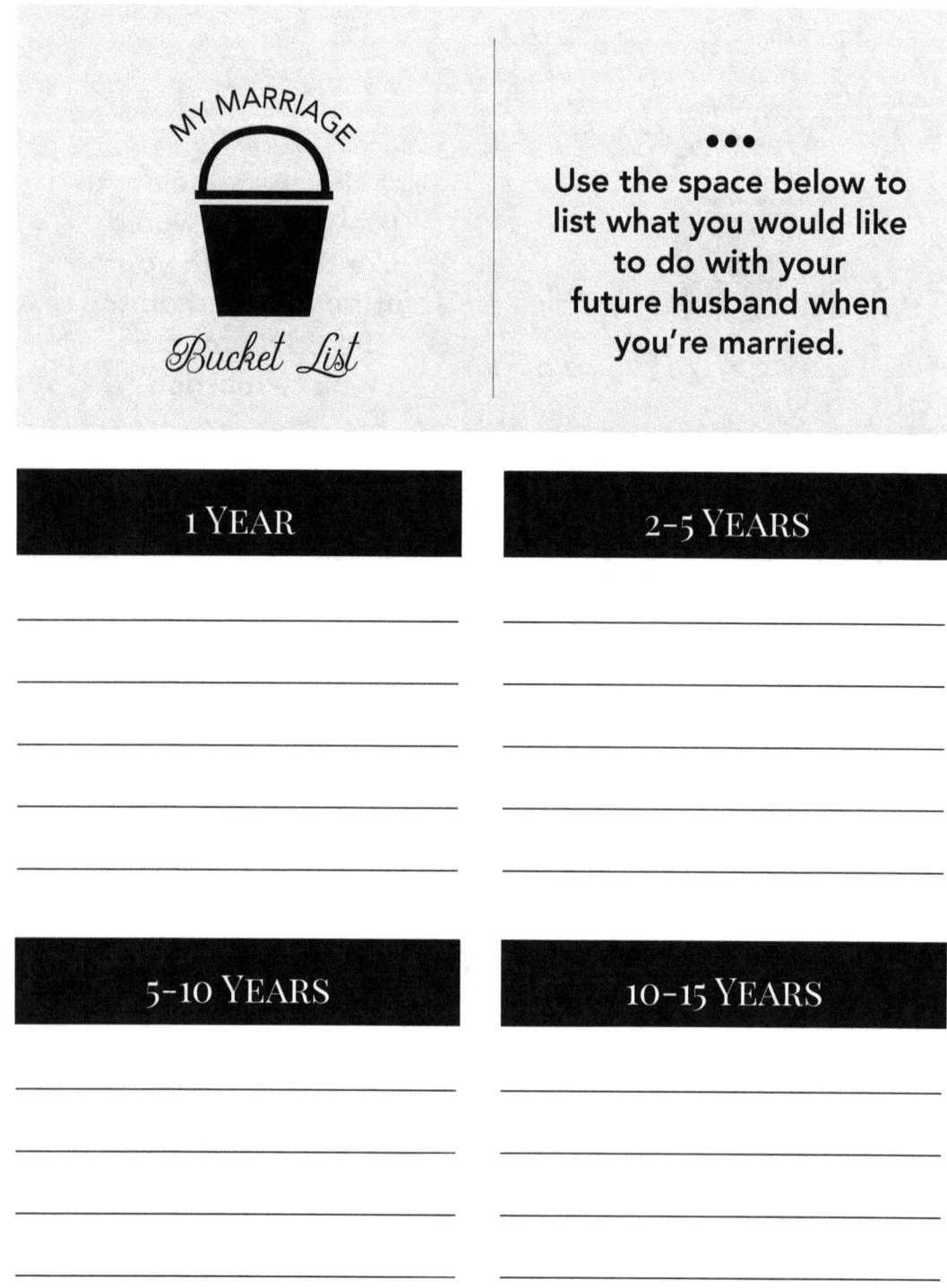

1 YEAR

_____
_____
_____
_____
_____

2-5 YEARS

_____
_____
_____
_____
_____

5-10 YEARS

_____
_____
_____
_____
_____

10-15 YEARS

_____
_____
_____
_____
_____

My Bucket Lists

•••
Use the space below to list what you would like to do with your future husband when you're married.

15-20 YEARS

20-25 YEARS

20-25 YEARS

25 YEARS & BEYOND

"Hope and preparation help build the future you see in your dreams and visions."

- Coach Tarsha Campbell

CHAPTER
12

MY HOPE CHEST

My Hope Chest

Things I Need at the Start of My Marriage

Create a list of the things you will need at the start of your marriage, such as items to set up your home and life with your future husband.

☐ _____   ☐ _____
☐ _____   ☐ _____
☐ _____   ☐ _____
☐ _____   ☐ _____
☐ _____   ☐ _____
☐ _____   ☐ _____
☐ _____   ☐ _____
☐ _____   ☐ _____
☐ _____   ☐ _____
☐ _____   ☐ _____
☐ _____   ☐ _____
☐ _____   ☐ _____

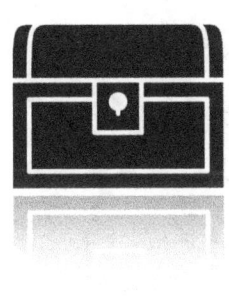

THINGS I NEED AT THE START OF MY MARRIAGE

Create a list of the things you will need at the start of your marriage, such as items to set up your home and life with your future husband.

- ☐ _____
- ☐ _____
- ☐ _____
- ☐ _____
- ☐ _____

Notes:

My Hope Chest

THINGS I NEED AT THE START OF MY MARRIAGE

Create a list of the things you will need at the start of your marriage, such as items to set up your home and life with your future husband.

- [ ] _____
- [ ] _____
- [ ] _____
- [ ] _____
- [ ] _____
- [ ] _____
- [ ] _____
- [ ] _____
- [ ] _____
- [ ] _____
- [ ] _____
- [ ] _____

- [ ] _____
- [ ] _____
- [ ] _____
- [ ] _____
- [ ] _____
- [ ] _____
- [ ] _____
- [ ] _____
- [ ] _____
- [ ] _____
- [ ] _____
- [ ] _____

My Hope Chest

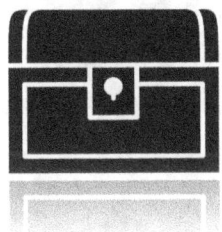

THINGS I NEED AT THE START OF MY MARRIAGE

Create a list of the things you will need at the start of your marriage, such as items to set up your home and life with your future husband.

- ☐ _____
- ☐ _____
- ☐ _____
- ☐ _____
- ☐ _____

Notes:

"A vow to purity is valuable and honorable to God. It is a vow of love to your beloved, even before he finds you. With this promise, you are saying you're willing to save a sacred part of yourself for him."

- Coach Tarsha Campbell

CHAPTER 13

MY VOW TO PURITY

"Holy Matrimony starts in your heart and actions way before you get the engagement ring and walk down the aisle to get married."

- Coach Tarsha Campbell

My Vow to Purity

Nothing is more attractive to a wise and suitable man searching for his future wife than a woman who has made the decision to save herself for her future husband.

Even if you have crossed the line and given away one of womanhood's most treasured possessions to someone other than your future husband, from this point on, you can make a vow to purity, embrace celibacy, and personally commit to saving yourself for the man who will call you his wife.

This vow is most impactful and honorable if you first make this commitment to God, as well as to your future husband. Holy Matrimony starts in your heart and actions way before you get the engagement ring and walk down the aisle to get married. Both parties involved in the relationship should be willing to make a commitment to save themselves for their future spouse. Also, both should wholeheartedly vow to God to refrain from sexual involvement with each other before they join in marriage before Him. This is His highest and best plan for the future bride and groom.

My Vow to Purity

•••
Use the following space to write a letter to God declaring your vow to purity.

Dear God,

I vow to...

My Vow to Purity

•••
Use the following space to write a letter to your future husband declaring your vow to purity.

Dear Future Husband,

I vow to...

"It's important that your words line up with what your heart desires. Negative words, thoughts, and self-talk can sabotage God's plans for your future as a married woman."

- Coach Tarsha Campbell

CHAPTER
14

31 Days of Affirmations

"Saying what you see
is key to making it your reality."

- Coach Tarsha Campbell

31 Days of Affirmations

It's important that your words line up with what your heart desires. Negative words, thoughts, and self-talk can sabotage God's plans for your future as a married woman.

Using the following space, write affirming, one-sentence declarations to your husband describing what type of wife you will be.

You can also use this section to write positive affirmations concerning the type of marriage you and your future husband will have.

Example #1:
I'm getting ready. I will be all God needs me to be for my future husband.

Example #2:
My future husband and I will have a happy marriage filled with tons of love and peace.

Once your affirmations are written, take time every day to declare them by faith until you see the manifestation of what you're speaking.

WHAT I SEE, DECLARE, & AFFIRM FOR MY FUTURE MARRIAGE.

DAY 01:

DAY 02:

DAY 03:

DAY 04:

What I See, Declare, & Affirm for My Future Marriage.

Day 05:

Day 06:

Day 07:

Day 08:

What I See, Declare, & Affirm for My Future Marriage.

Day 09:

Day 10:

Day 11:

Day 12:

What I See, declare, & affirm for my future marriage.

Day 13: _____

Day 14: _____

Day 15: _____

Day 16: _____

What I See, declare, & affirm for my future marriage.

Day 17:

Day 18:

Day 19:

Day 20:

What I See, declare, & affirm for my future marriage.

Day 21:

Day 22:

Day 23:

Day 24:

What I See, Declare, & Affirm for My Future Marriage.

Day 25:

Day 26:

Day 27:

Day 28:

What I See, Declare, & Affirm for My Future Marriage.

DAY 29: _____

DAY 30: _____

DAY 31: _____

NOTES: _____

"The entrance of Your words
gives light;
It gives understanding
to the simple.

- Psalm 119:130 (NKJV)

CHAPTER 15

Scripture Meditation For Preparation

*"The word of God is a treasure trove
of wisdom on how to have
a happy and successful life and marriage.
It's only a matter of
studying and applying what's been
shared to experience the best
God has purposed for
you and your future husband."*

- Coach Tarsha Campbell

Scripture Meditation For Preparation

God ordained marriage, and He takes this special covenant between a man and a woman seriously. This is why the subject of marriage and related issues are included in God's word.

As you prepare to be found by your future husband, you are encouraged to set aside quality time and meditate upon the following Scriptures.

Also, take the next step and write down what the Holy Spirit reveals to you. These Scriptures, and what is revealed by the Holy Spirit, will help to prepare your heart for your future spouse, your marriage, and your life together.

***

Let your time of meditation start with you expressing what you expect to gain as you spend time in God's word preparing for your spouse, marriage and life together.

What I expect to receive from God's word:

Scripture Meditation for Preparation

God's Desire to Create Help for Man

Genesis 2:18 (NKJV)

And the LORD God said, "[It is] not good that man should be alone; I will make him a helper comparable to him."

God Fulfills His Promise to Send Man Help

Genesis 2:21-24 (NKJV)

21 And the LORD God caused a deep sleep to fall on Adam, and he slept; and He took one of his ribs, and closed up the flesh in its place.

22 Then the rib which the LORD God had taken from man He made into a woman, and He brought her to the man.

23 And Adam said: "This [is] now bone of my bones And flesh of my flesh; She shall be called Woman, Because she was taken out of Man."

24 Therefore a man shall leave his father and mother and be joined to his wife, and they shall become one flesh.

A Wife: The Goodness of God Extended to Man

(Quick note: Check out how this Scripture reads in various biblical translations.)

Proverbs 18:22 (NKJV)

[He who] finds a wife finds a good [thing,] And obtains favor from the LORD.

Proverbs 18:22 (NLT)

The man who finds a wife finds a treasure, and he receives favor from the LORD.

Scripture Meditation for Preparation

An Understanding Wife Comes From the Lord

Proverbs 19:14 (NLT)

Fathers can give their sons an inheritance of houses and wealth, but only the Lord can give an understanding wife.

The Two Become One

Matthew 19:4-6 (NKJV)

4 And He answered and said to them, "Have you not read that He who made [them] at the beginning 'made them male and female,'

5 "and said, 'For this reason a man shall leave his father and mother and be joined to his wife, and the two shall become one flesh'?

6 "So then, they are no longer two but one flesh. Therefore what God has joined together, let not man separate."

Understanding the Impact of a Quarrelsome Wife

(Quick note: Check out how this Scripture reads in various biblical translations. Insightful!)

Proverbs 21:9 (NLT)

"It's better to live alone in the corner of an attic than with a quarrelsome wife in a lovely home."

Proverbs 21:9 (CEV)

It's better to stay outside on the roof of your house than to live inside with a nagging wife.

Scripture Meditation for Preparation

A Divine Setup for Protection and Blessings

Colossians 3:18-19 (NKJV)

18 Wives, submit to your own husbands, as is fitting in the Lord.

19 Husbands, love your wives and do not be bitter toward them.

Great Pattern for an Exceptional Wife

Proverbs 31:10-31 (NKJV)

10 Who can find a virtuous wife? For her worth [is] far above rubies.

11 The heart of her husband safely trusts her; So he will have no lack of gain.

12 She does him good and not evil All the days of her life.

13 She seeks wool and flax, And willingly works with her hands.

14 She is like the merchant ships, She brings her food from afar.

15 She also rises while it is yet night, And provides food for her household, And a portion for her maidservants.

16 She considers a field and buys it; From her profits she plants a vineyard.

17 She girds herself with strength, And strengthens her arms.

18 She perceives that her merchandise [is] good, And her lamp does not go out by night.

19 She stretches out her hands to the distaff, And her hand holds the spindle.

20 She extends her hand to the poor, Yes, she reaches out her hands to the needy.

21 She is not afraid of snow for her household, For all her household [is] clothed with scarlet.

22 She makes tapestry for herself; Her clothing [is] fine linen and purple.

23 Her husband is known in the gates, When he sits among the elders of the land.

24 She makes linen garments and sells [them,] And supplies sashes for the merchants.

25 Strength and honor [are] her clothing; She shall rejoice in time to come.

26 She opens her mouth with wisdom, And on her tongue [is] the law of kindness.

27 She watches over the ways of her household, And does not eat the bread of idleness.

28 Her children rise up and call her blessed; Her husband [also,] and he praises her:

29 "Many daughters have done well, But you excel them all."

30 Charm [is] deceitful and beauty [is] passing, But a woman [who] fears the LORD, she shall be praised.

31 Give her of the fruit of her hands, And let her own works praise her in the gates.

Scripture Meditation for Preparation

God Takes the Covenant of Marriage Seriously

Malachi 2:14-16 (NLT)

14 You cry out, "Why doesn't the LORD accept my worship?" I'll tell you why! Because the LORD witnessed the vows you and your wife made when you were young. But you have been unfaithful to her, though she remained your faithful partner, the wife of your marriage vows.

15 Didn't the LORD make you one with your wife? In body and spirit you are his. And what does he want? Godly children from your union. So guard your heart; remain loyal to the wife of your youth.

16 "For I hate divorce!" says the LORD, the God of Israel. "To divorce your wife is to overwhelm her with cruelty," says the LORD of Heaven's Armies. "So guard your heart; do not be unfaithful to your wife."

Submission Equals Spiritual Protection

Ephesians 5:22-25 (NKJV)

22 Wives, submit to your own husbands, as to the Lord.

23 For the husband is head of the wife, as also Christ is head of the church; and He is the Savior of the body.

24 Therefore, just as the church is subject to Christ, so [let] the wives [be] to their own husbands in everything.

25 Husbands, love your wives, just as Christ also loved the church and gave Himself for her.

Love Matters

1 Corinthians 13:1-3 (NKJV)

1 Though I speak with the tongues of men and of angels, but have not love, I have become sounding brass or a clanging cymbal.

2 And though I have [the gift of] prophecy, and understand all mysteries and all knowledge, and though I have all faith, so that I could remove mountains, but have not love, I am nothing.

3 And though I bestow all my goods to feed [the poor,] and though I give my body to be burned, but have not love, it profits me nothing.

What Love Looks Like

1 Corinthians 13:4-7 (NKJV)

4 Love suffers long [and] is kind; love does not envy; love does not parade itself, is not puffed up;

5 does not behave rudely, does not seek its own, is not provoked, thinks no evil;

6 does not rejoice in iniquity, but rejoices in the truth;

7 bears all things, believes all things, hopes all things, endures all things.

Marriage and Christ's Example

Ephesians 5:25-29 (NKJV)

25 Husbands, love your wives, just as Christ also loved the church and gave Himself for her,

26 that He might sanctify and cleanse her with the washing of water by the word,

27 that He might present her to Himself a glorious church, not having spot or wrinkle or any such thing, but that she should be holy and without blemish.

28 So husbands ought to love their own wives as their own bodies; he who loves his wife loves himself.

Scripture Meditation for Preparation

29 For no one ever hated his own flesh, but nourishes and cherishes it, just as the Lord [does] the church.

Rules of Engagement for Sexual Relations

1 Corinthians 7:1-5 (NLT)

1 Now regarding the questions you asked in your letter. Yes, it is good to abstain from sexual relations.

2 But because there is so much sexual immorality, each man should have his own wife, and each woman should have her own husband.

3 The husband should fulfill his wife's sexual needs, and the wife should fulfill her husband's needs.

4 The wife gives authority over her body to her husband, and the husband gives authority over his body to his wife.

5 Do not deprive each other of sexual relations, unless you both agree to refrain from sexual intimacy for a limited time so you can give yourselves more completely to prayer. Afterward, you should come together again so that Satan won't be able to tempt you because of your lack of self-control.

God's Expectations for Husbands

1 Peter 3:7 (BSB)

Husbands, in the same way, treat your wives with consideration as a delicate vessel, and with honor as fellow heirs of the gracious gift of life, so that your prayers will not be hindered.

Keys to a Successful Marriage

Ephesians 5:31-33 (NKJV)

31 "For this reason a man shall leave his father and mother and be joined to his wife, and the two shall become one flesh."

32 This is a great mystery, but I speak concerning Christ and the church.

33 Nevertheless let each one of you in particular so love his own wife as himself, and let the wife [see] that she respects [her] husband.

Making the Right Connection

2 Corinthians 6:14 (NKJV)

Do not be unequally yoked together with unbelievers. For what fellowship has righteousness with lawlessness? And what communion has light with darkness?

Characteristics of a Mature and Godly Wife

Colossians 3:12-17 (NKJV)

12 Therefore, as [the] elect of God, holy and beloved, put on tender mercies, kindness, humility, meekness, longsuffering;

13 bearing with one another, and forgiving one another, if anyone has a complaint against another; even as Christ forgave you, so you also [must do].

14 But above all these things put on love, which is the bond of perfection.

15 And let the peace of God rule in your hearts, to which also you were called in one body; and be thankful.

16 Let the word of Christ dwell in you richly in all wisdom, teaching and admonishing one another in psalms and hymns and spiritual songs, singing with grace in your hearts to the Lord.

17 And whatever you do in word or deed, [do] all in the name of the Lord Jesus, giving thanks to God the Father through Him.

An Effective Code of Action for Married Couples

1 Peter 4:8-10 (NKJV)

8 And above all things have fervent love for one another, for "love will cover a multitude of sins."

9 [Be] hospitable to one another without grumbling.

10 As each one has received a gift, minister it to one another, as good stewards of the manifold grace of God.

----- Bonus Insights -----

Plan, Prepare, Follow God's Lead

Proverbs 16:9 (NKJV)

A man's heart plans his way, But the LORD directs his steps.

God Knows What It's Like to be a Husband

Isaiah 54:5 (NLT)

For your Creator will be your husband; the LORD of Heaven's Armies is his name! He is your Redeemer, the Holy One of Israel, the God of all the earth.

Scripture Meditation for Preparation

Adultery Starts in the Heart

Matthew 5:27-28 (NKJV)

27 "You have heard that it was said to those of old, 'You shall not commit adultery.'

28 "But I say to you that whoever looks at a woman to lust for her has already committed adultery with her in his heart."

Honor God With Your Body

1 Corinthians 6:18-20 (NLT)

18 Run from sexual sin! No other sin so clearly affects the body as this one does. For sexual immorality is a sin against your own body.

19 Don't you realize that your body is the temple of the Holy Spirit, who lives in you and was given to you by God? You do not belong to yourself,

20 for God bought you with a high price. So you must honor God with your body.

The Value of Togetherness

Ecclesiastes 4:9-12 (NKJV)

9 Two [are] better than one, Because they have a good reward for their labor.

10 For if they fall, one will lift up his companion. But woe to him [who is] alone when he falls, For [he has] no one to help him up.

11 Again, if two lie down together, they will keep warm; But how can one be warm [alone?]

Scripture Meditation for Preparation

12 Though one may be overpowered by another, two can withstand him. And a threefold cord is not quickly broken.

A Powerful Position to Take in Life and as a Wife

1 Corinthians 16:13-14 (NKJV)

13 Watch, stand fast in the faith, be brave, be strong.

14 Let all [that] you [do] be done with love.

Scripture Meditation for Preparation

Make a note of your personal reflections.

Scripture Meditation for Preparation

Make a note of your personal reflections.

Scripture Meditation for Preparation

Make a note of your personal reflections.

"Dreaming ahead
puts you where
you want to be in the future."

- Coach Tarsha Campbell

CHAPTER
16

Dreaming Ahead:
Planning for Your Wedding Day

"Planning is a huge part of being a wife. Plan in faith. Plan intentionally."

- Coach Tarsha Campbell

Dreaming Ahead:
Planning for Your Wedding Day

You have envisioned and prepared for your future husband and marriage. Now take another leap of faith by planning for your wedding day.

This section isn't meant to give you a false sense that you're about to walk down the aisle. Instead, it is meant to help you remain conscious that the big day is coming as you continue to envision, dream, prepare, and believe in the process. Planning is a huge part of being a wife. Plan in faith. Plan intentionally.

So, as you continue to prepare and plan, make a note and list the wedding vendors that you want to remember when the BIG day arrives. You do believe it's coming, right? And while you're planning, start saving and creating a budget for your future wedding. Happy envisioning. Happy dreaming. Happy preparing. Happy planning!

Dreaming Ahead: Planning for Your Wedding Day

WEDDING PLANNERS

- ☐ _____
- ☐ _____
- ☐ _____
- ☐ _____
- ☐ _____

Notes:

Dreaming Ahead: Planning for Your Wedding Day

WEDDING OFFICIANTS

☐ _____

☐ _____

☐ _____

☐ _____

☐ _____

Notes:

Venues – Wedding Rehearsal

- ☐ _____
- ☐ _____
- ☐ _____
- ☐ _____
- ☐ _____

Notes:

Dreaming Ahead: Planning for Your Wedding Day

VENUES – WEDDING REHEARSAL DINNER

☐ _____

☐ _____

☐ _____

☐ _____

☐ _____

Notes:

Dreaming Ahead: Planning for Your Wedding Day

VENUES - BRIDAL SHOWER

- ☐ _____
- ☐ _____
- ☐ _____
- ☐ _____
- ☐ _____

Notes:

Dreaming Ahead: Planning for Your Wedding Day

VENUES – BACHELORETTE PARTY

- ☐ _____
- ☐ _____
- ☐ _____
- ☐ _____
- ☐ _____

Notes:

Dreaming Ahead: Planning for Your Wedding Day

VENUES – WEDDING CEREMONY

☐ _____

☐ _____

☐ _____

☐ _____

☐ _____

Notes:

Dreaming Ahead: Planning for Your Wedding Day

VENUES - RECEPTION

☐ _____

☐ _____

☐ _____

☐ _____

☐ _____

Notes:

Dreaming Ahead: Planning for Your Wedding Day

INVITATIONS - PRINTED

☐ _____

☐ _____

☐ _____

☐ _____

☐ _____

Notes:

Dreaming Ahead: Planning for Your Wedding Day

INVITATIONS - DIGITAL

- ☐ _____
- ☐ _____
- ☐ _____
- ☐ _____
- ☐ _____

Notes:

Dreaming Ahead: Planning for Your Wedding Day

DIGITAL WEDDING PLANNERS

☐ _____

☐ _____

☐ _____

☐ _____

☐ _____

Notes:

Dreaming Ahead: Planning for Your Wedding Day

WEDDING WEBSITE

☐ _____

☐ _____

☐ _____

☐ _____

☐ _____

Notes:

Wedding Attire

- ☐ _____
- ☐ _____
- ☐ _____
- ☐ _____
- ☐ _____

Notes:

Dreaming Ahead: Planning for Your Wedding Day

JEWELERS

- ☐ _____
- ☐ _____
- ☐ _____
- ☐ _____
- ☐ _____

Notes:

Food & Catering

- ☐ _____
- ☐ _____
- ☐ _____
- ☐ _____
- ☐ _____

Notes:

Dreaming Ahead: Planning for Your Wedding Day

BAKERS

- ☐ _____
- ☐ _____
- ☐ _____
- ☐ _____
- ☐ _____

Notes:

Music & Entertainment

- ☐ _____
- ☐ _____
- ☐ _____
- ☐ _____
- ☐ _____

Notes:

Dreaming Ahead: Planning for Your Wedding Day

LIGHTING

☐ _____
☐ _____
☐ _____
☐ _____
☐ _____

Notes:

Dreaming Ahead: Planning for Your Wedding Day

PHOTOGRAPHERS

☐ _____

☐ _____

☐ _____

☐ _____

☐ _____

Notes:

Dreaming Ahead: Planning for Your Wedding Day

VIDEOGRAPHERS

☐ _____

☐ _____

☐ _____

☐ _____

☐ _____

Notes:

Photo Booth

☐ _____

☐ _____

☐ _____

☐ _____

☐ _____

Notes:

Dreaming Ahead: Planning for Your Wedding Day

WEDDING ITEM RENTALS

- ☐ _____
- ☐ _____
- ☐ _____
- ☐ _____
- ☐ _____

Notes:

FLORISTS

☐ _____

☐ _____

☐ _____

☐ _____

☐ _____

Notes:

Dreaming Ahead: Planning for Your Wedding Day

LINENS

☐ _____

☐ _____

☐ _____

☐ _____

☐ _____

Notes:

Dreaming Ahead: Planning for Your Wedding Day

Decor

- ☐ _____
- ☐ _____
- ☐ _____
- ☐ _____
- ☐ _____

Notes:

Dreaming Ahead: Planning for Your Wedding Day

REGISTRY & GIFTS

☐ _____

☐ _____

☐ _____

☐ _____

☐ _____

Notes:

Dreaming Ahead: Planning for Your Wedding Day

WEDDING PARTY GIFTS

- ☐ _____
- ☐ _____
- ☐ _____
- ☐ _____
- ☐ _____

Notes:

Dreaming Ahead: Planning for Your Wedding Day

Transportation

- ☐ _____
- ☐ _____
- ☐ _____
- ☐ _____
- ☐ _____

Notes:

Dreaming Ahead: Planning for Your Wedding Day

HOTELS

- ☐ _____
- ☐ _____
- ☐ _____
- ☐ _____
- ☐ _____

Notes:

Dreaming Ahead: Planning for Your Wedding Day

HAIRSTYLISTS

☐ _____

☐ _____

☐ _____

☐ _____

☐ _____

Notes:

MAKE-UP ARTISTS

☐ _____

☐ _____

☐ _____

☐ _____

☐ _____

Notes:

Dreaming Ahead: Planning for Your Wedding Day

NAIL TECHS/SHOPS

☐ _____

☐ _____

☐ _____

☐ _____

☐ _____

Notes:

SEAMSTRESSES

☐ _____

☐ _____

☐ _____

☐ _____

☐ _____

Notes:

Dreaming Ahead: Planning for Your Wedding Day

TAILORS

- ☐ _____
- ☐ _____
- ☐ _____
- ☐ _____
- ☐ _____

Notes:

Dreaming Ahead: Planning for Your Wedding Day

PET SITTERS/BOARDERS

☐ _____

☐ _____

☐ _____

☐ _____

☐ _____

Notes:

Dreaming Ahead: Planning for Your Wedding Day

OTHER VENDORS

☐ _____

☐ _____

☐ _____

☐ _____

☐ _____

Notes:

Dreaming Ahead: Planning for Your Wedding Day

HONEYMOON

- ☐ _____
- ☐ _____
- ☐ _____
- ☐ _____
- ☐ _____

Notes:

Dreaming Ahead: Planning for Your Wedding Day

MISCELLANEOUS

☐ _____

☐ _____

☐ _____

☐ _____

☐ _____

Notes:

Dreaming Ahead: Planning for Your Wedding Day

WEDDING BUDGET WORKSHEET

The dreaming, preparing, and planning continues.
Let's work through some wedding cost projections. How much will your special day cost? How much should you be saving now?

Item	Budget	Actual
☐		
☐		
☐		
☐		
☐		
☐		
☐		
☐		
☐		
☐		

Dreaming Ahead: Planning for Your Wedding Day

	ITEM	BUDGET	ACTUAL
☐			
☐			
☐			
☐			
☐			
☐			
☐			
☐			
☐			
☐			
☐			
☐			
☐			
☐			
☐			
☐			

Dreaming Ahead: Planning for Your Wedding Day

	Item	Budget	Actual
☐			
☐			
☐			
☐			
☐			
☐			
☐			
☐			
☐			
☐			
☐			
☐			
☐			
☐			
☐			
☐			

Dreaming Ahead: Planning for Your Wedding Day

	ITEM	BUDGET	ACTUAL
☐			
☐			
☐			
☐			
☐			
☐			
☐			
☐			
☐			
☐			
☐			
☐			
☐			
☐			
☐			
☐			

"Learning from people who know will help you avoid unnecessary heartache and pain."

- Coach Tarsha Campbell

CHAPTER
17

ADVICE FOR A HAPPY MARRIED LIFE

Advice for a Happy Married Life

ADVICE FROM THOSE WHO KNOW

Identify and interview wives who have happy and successful marriages, asking the following question:

> What are some important things that single women should consider before marrying?

Wife:

ADVICE RECEIVED

Advice for a Happy Married Life

Wife:

ADVICE RECEIVED

Wife:

ADVICE RECEIVED

Advice for a Happy Married Life

ADVICE FROM THOSE WHO KNOW

Identify and interview wives who have happy and successful marriages, asking the following question:

> **What do you feel a husband needs the most?**

Wife:

ADVICE RECEIVED

Advice for a Happy Married Life

Wife:

ADVICE RECEIVED

Wife:

ADVICE RECEIVED

Advice for a Happy Married Life

ADVICE FROM TRUSTED MEN

Note: Out of respect for his wife, I encourage you NOT to ask a married man this question, unless he's a family member like your father, grandfather, or uncle you trust.

What qualities in a woman make her attractive and captivating?

Name:

ADVICE RECEIVED

Advice for a Happy Married Life

Name:

ADVICE RECEIVED

Name:

ADVICE RECEIVED

"Thanksgiving & gratitude keep the river of love and blessings flowing your way."

- Coach Tarsha Campbell

CHAPTER
18

I'm Glad You Found Me

*In everything give thanks; for this is
the will of God in Christ Jesus for you. (I Thessalonians 5:18, NKJV)*

•••

By faith, compose a prayer of thanksgiving and a declaration of gratitude because you have been found by your beloved husband.

Dear Beloved Husband,

I'm glad you found me... _____

_____

_____

_____

_____

_____

_____

_____

_____

_____

MEET THE AUTHOR

Tarsha L. Campbell is a dynamic Woman of Destiny! With this mandate, she humbly serves her community and the global community as an entrepreneur, international empowerment speaker, certified life and empowerment coach, business consultant, and mentor. Professionally and fondly known as Coach Tarsha, she is the author of nine popular books, with her most recent releases being *Unstuck: Your Next Step Coaching Guide & Interactive Journal* and *My Next Step Vision Board Dream Journal & Planner For Single Women Desiring Marriage.*

Coach Tarsha lives in the Central Florida area and has enjoyed a beautiful and fulfilling life with her beloved husband of 34 years, who she affectionately calls her "boyfriend." Coach Tarsha is passionate about empowering single women desiring marriage to experience the same marital bliss and fulfillment by helping them prepare to be the phenomenal wives their future husbands are searching for.

For info on how she empowers others, visit:

TarshaCampbellEmpowers.com

ReadyForMyHusband.com

Scan the code to access more empowerment resources.

www.ingramcontent.com/pod-product-compliance
Lightning Source LLC
LaVergne TN
LVHW081533070526
838199LV00005B/346